LYNX CHASE, HARES DASH

HUNTER AND HUNTED
ANIMAL SURVIVAL

JENS HAAKONSEN

PowerKiDS press.
New York

Published in 2018 by The Rosen Publishing Group, Inc.
29 East 21st Street, New York, NY 10010

First Edition

Editor: Theresa Morlock
Book Design: Reann Nye

Photo Credits: Cover (lynx), p. 18 Stanislav Duben/Shutterstock.com; cover (hare), p. 1 Michael Westerop/Shutterstock.com; p. 4 Tom Brakefield/DigitalVision/Getty Images; p. 5 Alexander Lysenko/Shutterstock.com; p. 6 ENEAU MARIE-PIERRE/ Shutterstock.com; pp. 7, 22 (hare) Jim Cumming/Shutterstock.com; p. 8 Howard Sandler/Shutterstock.com; p. 9 Michael Quinton/ Minden Pictures/Getty Images; p. 10 Richard Seeley/Shutterstock.com; p. 11 Copyright Michael Cummings/Moment/ Getty Images; pp. 12, 13 (bobcat) Don Mammoser/Shutterstock.com; p. 13 (Iberian lynx) Ramon Carretero/Shutterstock.com; p. 13 (Canada lynx) Warren Metcalf/Shutterstock.com; p. 13 (Eurasian lynx) PhotocechCZ/Shutterstock.com; pp. 14, 15, 20, 22 (lynx) Ondrej Prosicky/Shutterstock.com; p. 16 Debbie Steinhausser/Shutterstock.com; p. 17 Daniel J. Cox/Corbis Documentary/ Getty Images; p. 19 Philippe Henry/Design Pics/First Light/Getty Images; p. 21 Michio Hoshino/Minden Pictures/Getty Images.

Cataloging-in-Publication Data

Names: Haakonsen, Jens.
Title: Lynx chase, hares dash / Jens Haakonsen.
Description: New York : PowerKids Press, 2018. | Series: Hunter and hunted: animal survival | Includes index.
Identifiers: ISBN 9781508156710 (pbk.) | ISBN 9781508156642 (library bound) | ISBN 9781508156536 (6 pack)
Subjects: LCSH: Lynx–Juvenile literature. | Hares–Juvenile literature. | Predatory animals–Juvenile literature.
Classification: LCC QL737.C23 H33 2018 | DDC 599.75'3–dc23

Manufactured in the United States of America

CPSIA Compliance Information: Batch Batch #BS17PK: For Further Information contact Rosen Publishing, New York, New York at 1-800-237-9932

CONTENTS

LIFE IN THE TAIGA

The taiga, or boreal forest, is the largest land **biome** on Earth. It stretches over parts of Europe, Asia, and North America. Sitting just below the Arctic Circle, the taiga is known for its cold temperatures, frozen ground, and **muskegs**. The taiga has a long winter and a short summer. The winters are very cold, but the summers can get hot.

The taiga's forests are full of evergreen trees, such as firs, pines, and spruces. Snowshoe hares feed on twigs and bark there. Lynx feed on snowshoe hares.

WILDLIFE WISDOM

"Taiga" is the Russian word for "land of little sticks." The word "boreal" comes from Boreas, the ancient Greek god of the north wind. The word "boreal" is used to describe both these forests and the northern regions of the world in general.

The taiga includes parts of Alaska, Canada, Scandinavia, and Russia.

WHAT MAKES IT A SNOWSHOE?

Snowshoe hares have small bodies. Weighing only 2 to 4 pounds (0.9 to 1.8 kg), they are about 16 to 20 inches (40.6 to 50.8 cm) long. During winter their coats are white to blend in with their snowy surroundings. In the spring and summer they shed this coat and turn brown. The tips of their tall ears are black year-round.

Snowshoe hares have long back legs. Their large, furry toes allow them to walk on top of deep snow.

Snowshoe hares' feet work just like snowshoes do. That's how they got their name!

WILDLIFE WISDOM

Though hares and rabbits look quite similar, they are separate species, or kinds, of animals. Hares are usually larger than rabbits and have much longer ears. Hares live above ground and most rabbits build homes underground to live in.

MAD AS A MARCH HARE

Have you ever heard the expression "as mad as a March hare?" This saying is based on the behavior of male hares trying to attract female **mates**. To win a mate, male hares leap about wildly and chase females.

Snowshoe hares give birth to two or three **litters** of young each year with up to eight young per litter. Snowshoe hares' ability to have so many young is one of their greatest **adaptations**. Young hares are called leverets. Less than a month after they're born, leverets are able to take care of themselves.

Most snowshoe hares live for less than a year in the wild. However, some can live as long as five years.

HARES BEING HUNTED

Being able to reproduce quickly is necessary to the survival of the snowshoe hare species. In their boreal **ecosystem**, they are targeted by many predators. To avoid predators, hares feed at night. Snowshoe hares are herbivores, which means most of their diet is made up of grasses, shrubs, and other plants.

At their strongest, snowshoe hare populations can reach up to 3,400 hares per square mile in some places. Such high populations put a lot of pressure on boreal forest plants. Every 10 years or so, however, snowshoe hare populations drop very low.

Some causes of the snowshoe hare population swings include predation, starvation, and disease.

FIERCE FOES

Lynx depend on snowshoe hares as their main food source. Because of this, the lynx population cycle is closely linked to that of the snowshoe hare.

Lynx are carnivores, which means they only eat meat. They prey on hares, mice, squirrels, and birds. Lynx are very good hunters. They have powerful eyesight and are able to spot small prey, such as mice, from distances of up to 250 feet (762 m) away. They also have very strong hearing, which is aided by the tufts of hair inside their ears. Lynx hunt alone at night.

WILDLIFE WISDOM

There are four lynx species: the Iberian lynx, Canada lynx, Eurasian lynx, and bobcat. The lynx **habitat** ranges through parts of Europe, Asia, and North America. The Iberian lynx is at the highest risk of **extinction** due to loss of habitat and prey species.

People hunt lynx for their meat and beautiful fur. The Iberian lynx is the most **endangered** feline species in the world.

THE LOVELY LYNX

Lynx are medium-sized wildcats. They weigh 22 to 44 pounds (10 to 20 kg), with a body that's 32 to 40 inches (81.3 to 101.6 cm) long. Their short tail is 4 to 8 inches (10 to 20 cm) long and black at the tip.

Lynx have a bowed appearance because their back legs are longer than their front legs.

WILDLIFE WISDOM

Hunting animals illegally is called poaching. Poachers often hunt lynx because they wish to sell their beautiful fur. Lynx are also sometimes killed by farmers who see them as a threat to livestock.

Lynx are covered in warm, thick fur. Like the snowshoe hare, they have fuzzy, wide-toed feet. These feet allow them to walk on snow with ease. Lynx have long, white tufts of fur around their face. They have spotted coats, which are usually gray, brownish, or reddish in color.

A LYNX'S LIFE

Lynx keep to themselves except when they look for mates. Males and females locate each other through territories marked with their scent. They communicate by yowling, grunting, and purring.

Females have their kittens in dens. Unlike snowshoe hares, lynx only give birth once a year. There are one to four kittens in each litter. Mother lynx care for their kittens until the young lynx are about a year old. Adult lynx face many dangers, including starvation, habitat **destruction**, and being hit by cars. In the wild, lynx can live up to 15 years.

Mother lynx teach their kittens how to hunt hares and other prey.

FACE-OFF!

What happens when a quick snowshoe hare faces a clever lynx? Lynx use their sharp eyesight to spot snowshoe hares from great distances. They stalk their prey by creeping toward them quietly. Lynx are talented climbers and sometimes **ambush** hares by leaping down on them from trees or rocks.

Snowshoe hares can dash at speeds up to 27 miles (43.5 km) per hour. They can jump 10 feet (3 m) in a single hop! Snowshoe hares sometimes escape lynx by running in a zigzag pattern or leaping into water, where they can use their large feet to swim away.

Lynx can run at speeds up to 40 miles (64.4 km) per hour when chasing their prey. Snowshoe hares need to change directions to avoid becoming lunch.

KEEPING THE BALANCE

If a lynx manages to catch a snowshoe hare, the hare doesn't stand a chance. A lynx's weight, powerful jaws, and sharp teeth give it a strong advantage, allowing it to overpower the hare by choking it. A hare's best chance for survival lies in blending in with its surroundings to avoid being spotted or dashing away.

Snowshoe hare and lynx species need each other to survive. Without lynx to keep their populations in check, snowshoe hares can take over an ecosystem and run out of food. Without hares to feed on, lynx can starve.

The close population cycles of snowshoe hares and lynx show how **interdependent** the two species truly are.

WILDLIFE WISDOM

Taiga ecosystems are put at risk by **climate change**. As global temperatures rise, the frozen ground begins to thaw. This creates more muskegs than is healthy. Warming temperatures also draw nonnative species to the taiga. These species compete for food and shelter and native species suffer.

TEAM LYNX VS. TEAM HARE

Which animal would you root for in the battle for survival? Will the snowshoe hare's camouflage and **agility** save it from the lynx's speed and strength?

Humans are the greatest threat to both lynx and snowshoe hares. As cities expand and human populations grow, lynx and hare habitats become smaller and the animals come into contact with people more often. Two such closely linked species are put at risk by changes in their ecosystem. What will the future hold for this hunter and hunted pair?

GLOSSARY

adaptation: A change in an animal that helps it survive better in its environment.

agility: The ability to move quickly and easily.

ambush: To attack by surprise from a hiding place.

biome: A large community of plants and animals that occupies a certain type of region.

climate change: Change in Earth's weather caused by human activity.

destruction: Great damage or ruin.

ecosystem: A natural community of living and nonliving things.

endangered: In danger of dying out.

extinction: The state of no longer existing.

habitat: The natural home for plants, animals, and other living things.

interdependent: When two things rely on one another.

litter: A group of baby animals born to a mother animal at one time.

mate: A partner for making babies, or to come together to make babies.

muskeg: A North American swamp or bog covered in water and moss.

INDEX

WEBSITES

Due to the changing nature of Internet links, PowerKids Press has developed an online list of websites related to the subject of this book. This site is updated regularly. Please use this link to access the list: www.powerkidslinks.com/handh/lynx